HISTORY AND GEOGRAPHY 606
SEVEN SOUTH AMERICA

CONTENTS

Author: **Bess Morton**

Editor-in-Chief: Richard W. Wheeler, M.A.Ed.

Editor: Elizabeth Loeks Bouman

Consulting Editor: J. Howard Stitt, Th.M., Ed.D.

Revision Editor: Alan Christopherson, M.S.

Alpha Omega Publications®

804 N. 2nd Ave. E., Rock Rapids, IA 51246-1759

SEVEN SOUTH AMERICAN COUNTRIES

The seven southern countries of South America to be studied in this LIFEPAC® differ in many ways from the countries in the north. Only one, Ecuador, is crossed by the equator. All seven southern countries touch the jungles of the inland. Most of them spread out into colder, harsher climates. The Andes Mountains become higher as they range southward along the western coast of South America. They descend sharply into the ocean at the extreme southern tip of the continent. These southern countries also share some events of history. All have had stormy periods since they became democracies, and most have military presidents. In 1980, however, Peru elected a civilian president. Other countries, like Argentina, are trying to change, but the task is difficult.

OBJECTIVES

Read these objectives. The objectives tell you what you should be able to do when you have successfully completed this LIFEPAC.

When you have finished this LIFEPAC, you should be able to:

1. Describe the geography of each of the seven countries in this LIFEPAC.
2. Give an account of the background and the lifestyle of the people living in each country.
3. Relate how each country was started and how it has grown to the present.
4. Name the capital of each country and at least one more city.
5. Name the principal resource or resources of each country and the major industries that have grown from these resources.

VOCABULARY

Study these new words. Learning the meanings of these words is a good study habit and will improve your understanding of this LIFEPAC.

abound (u bound'). Plentiful.

blight (blīt). A disease of plants.

captor (kap' tur). A person who takes or holds a prisoner.

complex (kum pleks'). A group of buildings, units, and so forth.

conflict (kon' flikt). A disagreement, fight, or struggle.

conquest (kon' kwest). An act of conquering; the thing, person, or land conquered.

despot (des' put). Ruler having unlimited power; tyrant.

docile (dos' ul). Easily managed; obedient.

erupt (i rupt'). Burst forth suddenly.

estuary (es' chù er' ē). A broad mouth of a river into which the tide flows.

extension (ek sten' shun). The act of stretching or enlarging; increase in length.

guerrilla (gu ril' u). A person engaged in irregular warfare.

historical (his tôr' u kul). Of or having to do with history.

initiate (i nish' ē āt). Be the first one to start, set going, or begin.

isolate (ī' su lāt). Place apart; separate from others.

leisure (lē' zhur). Time free from required work.

oppress (u pres'). Govern harshly; keep down unjustly.

originate (u rij' u nāt). Cause to be, invent, come into being, or arise.

porcelain (pôr' su lin). A very fine earthenware; dish or other object made of this material.

repeal (ri pēl'). Do away with; withdraw; rescind; annul.

retain (ri tān'). Continue to have or hold; keep.

species (spē' shēz). A group of animals or plants having the same characteristics.

staple (stā' pul). Most important basic food; principal article grown or manufactured in a place.

urban (ėr' bun). Having to do with cities.

viceroy (vīs' roi). A person ruling a country under directions from the king or sovereign.

Note: All vocabulary words in this LIFEPAC appear in **boldface** print the first time they are used. If you are unsure of the meaning when you are reading, study the definitions given.

Pronunciation Key: hat, āge, cãre, fär; let, ēqual, tėrm; it, īce; hot, ōpen, ôrder; **oi**l; **ou**t; cup, pùt, rüle; **ch**ild; lo**ng**; **th**in; /TH/ for **th**en; /zh/ for mea**s**ure; /u/ represents /a/ in **a**bout, /e/ in tak**e**n, /i/ in penc**i**l, /o/ in lem**o**n, and /u/ in circ**u**s.

I. ECUADOR, PERU, AND BOLIVIA

Ecuador, Peru, and Bolivia share enough similarities in geography, history, and people to be one large country. All three were a part of one nation devoted to the Sun God during the prehistoric days of the Inca civilization. Over the years they have become divided into the countries that exist today. The people of each country are proud of their own heritage. You will study ways Ecuador, Peru, and Bolivia are alike. Then you will study each country separately.

SECTION OBJECTIVES

Review these objectives. When you have completed this section, you should be able to:

1. Describe the geography of Ecuador, Peru, and Bolivia.
2. Give an account of the background and the lifestyle of the people living in each country.
3. Relate how each country was started and how it has grown to the present.
4. Name the capital of each country and at least one other major city.
5. Name the principal resource or resources of each country and the major industries that have grown from these resources.

Restudy these words.

abound	despot	retain
blight	docile	species
captor	erupt	staple
complex	oppress	viceroy
conquest	originate	

GEOGRAPHY

In this section you will study the Andes Mountains. You will also study the general regional traits, waterways, and wildlife of the countries of the Andes region.

Mountains. The Andes Mountains (or *Sierras* as the South Americans call them) spread down from the north into Ecuador. In Ecuador the mountains are divided into two high ranges. One long line of ranges is called "The Avenue of Volcanoes." Several peaks **erupt** lava from time to time. Mount Cotopaxi is the highest "steaming" mountain in the world. Whenever volcanoes are active, we know the earth in that place has not yet settled permanently. Earthquakes often occur in such areas, as they do in Ecuador.

The Andes go on down through Peru. In Peru they are higher. Mount Hauscarán, at 22,202 feet, is one of the tallest peaks in the world. Between the mountain ranges, the plateaus are elevated also.

The mountains and plateaus of the Andes in the west-southwest border of Bolivia are very high and have extended to their widest point. In Bolivia the Andes Mountains are nearly four hundred miles wide in places. Three ranges, or *cordilleras,* have formed: the Cordillera Occidental (west), the Cordillera Central, and the Cordillera Oriental (east). At the northern end of the Cordillera Central is the Cordillera Real (royal). These ranges are full of glaciers, and their peaks reach extreme heights. The plateaus between the mountain ranges are also extremely high. The plateaus in Bolivia and Peru are called *altiplanos* (high plains). People who live and work on these *altiplanos* develop large chests and lungs. Lungs enlarge in order to absorb the small amount of oxygen available in the high altitudes.

Complete these statements by writing the correct words in the blanks.

1.1 The Andes mountains divide into _____ high ranges in Ecuador.

1.2 Mount Cotopaxi is called the highest _____ mountain in the world.

1.3 Areas that have volcanoes usually have _____ as well.

1.4 In Bolivia the Andes Mountains are nearly _____ miles wide in places.

1.5 In Bolivia the Andes Mountains have formed _____ ranges.

1.6 The plateaus in Bolivia and Peru are called _____ because they are so high.

1.7 People who live and work in the Andes develop _____ chests and lungs.

Eastern regions. The Spanish word for east is *oriente. Oriente* is the name the western countries of South America give to the low jungle areas that flatten out from the foot of the east side of the Andes. *Selva* is another name for this area. Low bushes and vines grow thickly in the selva. The weather is mostly hot and humid. In Ecuador the jungle is fairly wide, but in Peru the jungle is the size of Texas. Bolivia's lowlands take up almost three-fourths of the country. However, to the southeast, the jungle terrain begins to develop into the *Gran Chaco* (large swamp) that extends into Paraguay and even to Argentina.

Bolivia has two eastern regions. The first, part of the Gran Chaco just mentioned, is the Oriente-Chaco. The second is the *Yungas,* located on the hillsides of the mountains between the jungle and the high peaks. These eastern slopes are green and fertile, good for farming.

Western regions. Only Ecuador and Peru have western, or coastal, regions located between the Andes and the Pacific Ocean. Bolivia has no seacoast. The mountains form its western border.

Ecuador's coastline, especially in the south, is full of fertile valleys suitable for growing bananas and cocoa.

Peru's coastal region is a desert. Even the Andes mountains facing the ocean in Peru are barren. Two factors contribute to this condition. One factor is the mountains, which are so high in Peru that the warm, damp winds of the inland jungles cannot reach the coastline. The second factor is the Peru Current.

The Peru (or Humboldt) Current in the Pacific Ocean makes a huge circle. Starting far out in the ocean, it sweeps up the South American west coast beginning at the level of north Chile. It continues up the length of Peru. It then turns out into the Pacific again at the southern border of Ecuador. Above the Current are Ecuador's fertile valleys. Peru's coast, along the Current's path, is dry, having no rain, only occasional mists. The climate is right for desert plants, such as cotton, to be grown on Peru's coastal plain. The cold air of the Current, however, makes the weather surprisingly cool.

Write *eastern* **or** *western* **in the blank in front of each statement.**

1.8 _____ The Spanish word for it is *oriente.*

1.9 _____ These are coastal regions located between the Andes mountains and the Pacific Ocean.

1.10 _____ Fertile valleys in Ecuador suitable for growing bananas and cocoa.

1.11 _____ Peru's coastal region is a desert.

1.12 _____ Selva is a name for the low jungle areas at the foot of the Andes.

1.13 _____ The weather is mostly hot and humid.

1.14 _____ Peru's coast, along which the Peru Currents flows, has no rain, only occasional mist, but it is cool.

1.15 _____ Another name for the Peru Current is the Humboldt Current.

Galápagos Islands. Off of Ecuador's coast, about six hundred miles westward across the Pacific Ocean, lie the Galápagos Islands. These islands are owned by the country of Ecuador. Full of rocks and natural springs, they contain so many **species** of wildlife that scientists go there to study.

Rivers and other waterways. The Guayas River of Ecuador is wide at its mouth as it empties into the Pacific. Ocean-going ships can travel up the Guayas fifty miles to the city of Guayaquil. From there smaller boats can navigate on other rivers forty to eighty miles further inland. To the north of Ecuador, the Esmeraldas River can be navigated two hundred miles inland. On the east side of Ecuador's mountains, countless rivers are formed that eventually meet the Amazon River.

In Peru's Oriente, the Amazon's headwaters begin near the city of Iquitos. The water is so deep and so wide that ocean-going ships can come up the Amazon thirty-five hundred miles to the city, making it an "Atlantic Ocean seaport" for Peru. This fact is worth noting because Iquitos actually is only two hundred miles from the Pacific Ocean.

Lake Titicaca lies on an altiplano between Bolivia and Peru. Lake Titicaca is the highest navigable lake in the world. Being navigable makes it an important means of transportation and commerce for both countries.

Wildlife. Wildlife **abounds** everywhere in all three countries. In the Oriente, huge snakes, pumas, tapirs, and beautiful birds can be found. The ocean is full of tuna, shrimp, lobster, and crayfish. Fishermen enjoy catching twenty to thirty-pound trout in the lakes and rivers. Trout weighing one hundred twenty pounds have been reported in Lake Titicaca. On the Galápagos Islands, besides wild horses, wild dogs, and wild cattle left over from the days of the conquerors, there live animals such as giant tortoises, iguanas, albatrosses, cormorants, and pelicans. The finches that dwell in Galápagos have been the subject of many scientific writings. In the high Andes are condors and falcons.

The llama and its three cousins, the vicuña, the guanaco, and the alpaca, are symbols of Peru. These animals exist in other South American countries, but Peru makes the most use of them. They are related to the camel. The vicuña has very fine wool, but the animals hide in the mountains and are hard to find, so the supply of vicuña wool is scarce. Alpaca wool is in much demand all over the world for sweaters.

The llama is Peru's beast of burden. Many families own one or more, making spoiled pets of some of them. Being small, the llama cannot carry as heavy a load as a horse can. The llama is a **docile** animal, however, that can store water within itself for a long period of time. This trait makes it useful for work in the desert areas or wherever water is scarce. Llamas are used for food, too. The meat is sometimes stretched and dried in the sun. The Indians have always called this *charqui* (char key). *Jerky* that the pioneers in the United States made from beef was named after the South American *charqui*. Llama wool is heavy, suitable for thick blankets and coats.

Classify the words under the proper heading.

WORDS

albatrosses	llamas	tapirs
condors	lobsters	tortoises
crayfish	pelicans	tuna
falcons	pumas	wild cattle
finches	shrimp	wild dogs
iguanas	snakes	wild horses

1.16	Oriente	Andes	Seacoast	Galápagos
	_____	_____	_____	_____
	_____	_____	_____	_____
	_____	_____	_____	_____
	_____	_____	_____	_____
	_____	_____	_____	_____
	_____	_____	_____	_____

Find the antonyms for these words in the paragraphs on wildlife.

1.17
   a. plentiful _____
   b. empty _____
   c. midget _____
   d. die _____
   e. least _____

   f. coarse _____
   g. light _____
   h. thin _____
   i. unruly _____

Write _true_ or _false_ in the blank in front of each statement.

1.18 _____ The Rocky Mountain range runs through Ecuador, Peru, and Bolivia.

1.19 _____ All three of these countries touch the interior jungles.

1.20 _____ Peru has an "Atlantic seaport."

1.21 _____ The llama is related to the camel.

1.22 _____ The Andes Mountains are narrow in Bolivia.

1.23 _____ The llama family of animals are never raised for pets.

1.24 _____ The coastline of Peru is green with forests.

1.25 _____ Lake Titicaca produces no trout.

Complete this map activity.

1.26 On the work map in the back of your LIFEPAC, mark these areas: the Andes Mountain ranges, the Galápagos Islands, the jungle areas, and the coastal area. You may wish to color these with crayon or colored pencil.

1.27 Indicate the approximate course of the Peru Current in the Pacific Ocean, and mark the Guayas River and the Esmeraldas River in Ecuador.

1.28 Mark the city of Iquitos in Peru and the Amazon River.

1.29 Draw in Lake Titicaca between Peru and Bolivia. You will need to look at the sample map in your LIFEPAC or a wall map to be able to do this activity well.

Teacher check _____
                                 Initial   Date

PEOPLE

Most of the population of these three countries is Indian. You will study their schools, recreations, languages, religions, food, and clothing.

A Colorado Indian of Ecuador

Indians. Ecuador, Peru, and Bolivia are often referred to as Indian countries. Most of the people are either pure-blood Indians or mestizos (Indian and Spanish mixed). Many of them are Quechuas (ke´ choo uhs), descendants of the great prehistoric Inca tribes. In Bolivia, especially around Lake Titicaca, live descendants of tribes that were in Bolivia much earlier than the Incas.

Of course, each country has immigrant people or descendants of immigrants, including American, Japanese, Africans, and Europeans. These people form small minorities.

The men in the Colorado Indian tribe (the "red ones") of Ecuador color their hair red and plaster it with mud. This practice gives them the appearance of wearing red skull caps.

Jungle Indians of any tribe live within their own culture. They have little to do with "civilization." One or two tribes will have nothing at all to do with any other human beings. The Auca Indians in the jungles of Ecuador are fierce. In 1956 they killed five Protestant missionaries who thought they had befriended them. Relatives of the slain missionaries still are trying to reach out to the Auca. They have already succeeded in some ways. Many Aucas have been converted since the killings, including the men who killed the missionaries. Elizabeth Elliott, the wife of one of the men who was killed went back to live among the Aucas. She took her little girl with her and loved the Aucas for Christ's sake. Many have opened their hearts to Christ's love and salvation.

Luke 23:34 tells us that Jesus cried out to God about those who crucified him, "Father, forgive them; for they know not what they do." As a fellow Christian, perhaps you will want to pray for all Indians of South America that they, too, will open their hearts to the message of God's love and salvation.

Schools. Ecuador, Peru, and Bolivia all have laws to make children from six to twelve or from seven to fourteen go to school. But the laws are difficult to enforce. In 1900 Ecuador imported European teachers. By now most children in Ecuador attend primary school. A few of them go on to high school and college.

In Peru few schools exist. The people often are too poor to afford school clothes for their children.

Bolivia tries very hard to provide an education to all who need it. Only about half of the children attend school. In areas where there are not enough textbooks, however, the teacher reads the lesson from her book to the class. The children write down what she says and memorize it.

Recreation. *Futbol* (soccer) is a favorite sport in Ecuador, Peru, and Bolivia. Bullfighting is popular too. In Peru, many people sand ski on the beaches. Children like to shoot firecrackers on New Year's Day.

Boats Made from the Reeds of Lake Titicaca

Near Lake Titicaca, for pleasure and for work, men make boats and sails of the reeds—or bulrushes—of the *tortora* plant. The boats last only a few months, but plenty of bulrushes remain to make others.

The women of Bolivia are seen very often with spindles in their hands. They carry them everywhere to spin yarn from sheep's wool, or wool from the llama, the alpaca, or even the vicuña. Sometimes the women dye the wools bright colors before they spin them.

Festivals are celebrated for many things. In Bolivia the people make their own musical instruments out of reeds and bamboo. They make drums, mouth organs, guitars, and horns. People paint huge masks for themselves.

Religion. In all three countries festivals, except for patriotic ones, are related to the Roman Catholic Church. Most of the people belong to this church. Statues of Christ are put on the hills beside many villages to give the town a blessing. Celebrations sometimes include primitive traditions from the Indian religions.

Protestant missionaries are active in these countries. Sometimes missionaries serve in the jungles. Often two of them together set up their own hut near a native village. Some of them translate the Bible, some help the poor and the sick. All of them teach the Indians, when they are able, about God's love through Jesus Christ.

In rural villages away from the jungles, in the plateaus and altiplanos, missionaries go to teach about Jesus. They set up **complexes** which may include schools or medical clinics. Whenever the people of the towns have a festival, the missionaries and their families gather together with friends they have made from the town and have their own party and songfest. Sometimes they hold an all night prayer vigil.

In Psalm 137:4 the writer asks, "How shall we sing the Lord's song in a strange land?" The missionaries sing easily although they are far from home. They have a joyous message in their hearts.

Language. Spanish is the official language for Ecuador, Peru, and Bolivia. English is a second language, especially for conducting government business with other countries. Most of the people, however, also speak the Quechuan Indian dialects, as well as other Indian tongues.

Food. Ecuadoreans use many spices in their food. Naranjilla (little orange) juice is served there also. Chocolate drinks from their own home-grown cocoa beans are supposed to be the best anywhere.

We tend to think of potatoes as coming from Ireland and pumpkins from North America. But potatoes, squash, corn, pumpkins, and peanuts **originated** in this part of the world, especially in Peru and

Bolivia. The conquerors took samples of the "strange" food back to their European homes. From there they were grown and taken to other places. Potatoes are still the **staple** of the Quechua diet.

In the jungles, manioc, cooked several ways, is the basis for meals. In the United States, people eat tapioca which comes from the same plant as manioc.

Clothing. Clothing must be warm and heavy for the cold plateaus. Women wear circular skirts. The more layers of skirts a woman wears, the wealthier she is. Men wear colorful ponchos over their pants and shirts. Everybody wears hats. The women like round derby hats. Some men wear a *chullo,* a knit cap with ear flaps.

 Write *true* **or** *false.*

1.30 _____ The Colorado Indians are called the "red ones."
1.31 _____ Today's Quechua Indians are descendants of the ancient Incas.
1.32 _____ Jungle Indians often shop in the cities.
1.33 _____ Five missionaries live with the Auca Indians.
1.34 _____ Headhunters plaster their hair with mud.

 Match the words and phrases.

1.35 _____ potatoes
1.36 _____ European teachers
1.37 _____ students in Bolivia
1.38 _____ *futbol*
1.39 _____ derby hats
1.40 _____ boats on Titicaca
1.41 _____ firecrackers
1.42 _____ llamas
1.43 _____ spindles
1.44 _____ reeds and bamboo
1.45 _____ bright colors
1.46 _____ 6-12, 7-14
1.47 _____ chocolate drinks
1.48 _____ conquerors

a. musical instruments
b. took sample potatoes back home
c. related to camels
d. made of bulrushes
e. home-grown cocoa beans
f. memorize lessons
g. New Year's Day
h. spin yarn from wool
i. ages for going to school
j. manioc
k. Ecuador
l. yarn dyes
m. soccer
n. staple of Quechuan diet
o. Quechua women

Write in the blanks the correct word to complete the sentence.

1.49   Indian traditions are sometimes included in Roman Catholic

     _____ .

1.50   The official language of Ecuador, Peru, and Bolivia is _____ .

1.51   Indian _____ also are spoken.

1.52   The first _____ were grown in Peru and Ecuador.

1.53   Clothing must be _____ for the high plateaus.

1.54   In the jungles, Protestant missionaries set up their own _____

     near the Indian village.

HISTORY

The Indian countries, Ecuador, Peru, and Bolivia, are most famous for the reminders of the Inca empire which still exist there. You will study the Incas and learn about the men who conquered them. Although these countries were later freed from Spanish rule, a struggle to understand and practice democracy continues today.

Inca civilization. The Incas had no written language. Little is known today about them except word-of-mouth legend and what can be learned from ruins. The ruins of their cities and roads show how well they could build. Writings by Spanish conqueror-historians have given us a few accounts of the Incas at the time of the Spanish **conquest**.

The Incas were the last of a long line of vast Indian civilizations that centered in Peru. The Incas worshiped the sun god. By the middle of the fifteenth century (around 1450), the Incas had completed the conquest of all the other existing Indian tribes of western South America. It had taken them at least two centuries to complete the conquest. Each of the tribes conquered was allowed to **retain** its own culture. The **captors**, however, insisted that all worship the sun god. Everyone worked and lived for the King of the Incas, who, his subjects felt, represented the sun god.

The city of Cuzco, toward the south of Peru, was the Inca capital. Though they had not yet learned about the wheel, the Incas somehow hauled huge stone blocks to build their temples and palaces. The stones were laid in such a way that earthquakes have not destroyed the Inca walls to this day. Buildings put by conquerors on top of the ancient walls have crumbled several times. The Incas mined gold and silver, which was used to plate the building blocks.

Great stone walls were built beside fine highways that were used for marching troops, running messengers, or transporting goods by llamas. One stone-paved highway was 3,250 miles long. Another was 2,520 miles.

Farming and art were also important to the Incas. Crops were watered by a complicated irrigation system. The Inca weaving was finer than any present-day weaving. Inca pottery was beautiful.

The Inca government was well organized, but because one king did not name a strong son for his successor, the power of the monarchy began to decline.

Complete these statements.

1.55 The Incas had no _____ language.

1.56 The Incas worshiped the _____ .

1.57 The Incas had finished conquering all the other existing Indian tribes of western South America by about _____ .

1.58 The Inca capital was _____ .

1.59 Often the walls were plated with a. _____ and b. _____ , which the Incas mined.

1.60 Crops were watered by a complicated _____ system.

Conquest of the Incas. In 1532, the Spaniard, Francisco Pizzaro, took an expedition to Inca territory. He captured the Inca leaders by trickery. He and his men robbed and looted Inca palaces and temples, mainly in Cuzco. The gold plates from the walls were sent to Spain. On the foundations of the buildings they had ruined, the Spaniards built palaces and rich cathedrals. They burned and robbed so much that in Ecuador only one Inca carving remains.

Peru has most of what has survived of the Inca civilization. High in the plateaus of Peru is one entire city that Pizzaro never found. Discovered by a senator from the United States in 1911, its name is Machu Picchu.

Colonial period. After Pizzaro's conquest, the countries of Ecuador, Peru, and Bolivia were taken over by Spanish **viceroys**. Provinces were ruled by Spaniards from Spain. Creoles (full-blooded Spaniards born in the new country) and all others were severely **oppressed**. Indians that did not flee to the jungle were made slaves.

Spain considered the new country a "bank of gold." She was afraid of losing her new-found riches in South America. For nearly three hundred years Spain gave no freedom to her subjects.

Liberation. José de San Martín (mar teen) from Argentina, had taken his soldiers across the Andes to liberate Chile. When he finished there, he went north with his army.

In 1821 he defeated the Spanish in Lima, Peru. He was asked to unfurl the first national flag. San Martín defeated the Spanish in other battles. He became well loved, and was considered the liberator of the southern half of South America.

In the meantime Simón Bolívar had freed Venezuela, Columbia, and Ecuador from the Spanish. Now Bolívar was on his way south to Peru. Obviously, problems would arise with two liberators in one country. At a famous meeting between the two in Guayaquil, Ecuador, Bolívar and San Martín agreed to let Bolívar continue the battles. After saying farewell to his friends in a speech at Peru, San Martín went home to a poor welcome in Argentina. He went to Europe and died an unhappy man.

José de Sucre, one of Bolívar's generals, fought more battles to free Ecuador and Bolivia than Bolívar did, but is not as well known as Bolívar.

Bolívar's army defeated the Spanish completely in 1825. Bolívar returned to Colombia where he, too, died unhappily.

Years of democracy. Since liberation, the Indian countries have had democratic constitutions. Democracy has not come easily. Frequent changes have been made in the constitutions. Wars with neighboring countries have been costly.

In 1879, twenty-five years after democracy began, Peru fought the War of the Pacific with Bolivia and Chile over nitrates and fertilizer. Bolivia lost her seaport and coastline in the final peace settlement.

Almost sixty years later Bolivia fought another war (1928–1935). The Gran Chaco in the Oriente was the disputed land this time. Argentina and Paraguay were the enemies. Bolivia lost much territory again.

In all three countries, many presidents elected to office became dictators, ruling the country like **despots**, often with cruelty. Other presidents were democratic, helping the people to better lives and freedom.

In 1978 each country except Bolivia had a president elected from the armed forces. The presidents appoint military officers to be in their cabinets. However, in 1993, Bolivia held a civilian, democratic election.

In 1979, Ecuador returned to democratic elections, and in 1980, Peru also returned to a civilian, democratic government.

In all three countries, everyone over 18 years of age must vote, by law.

 Write *true* **or** *false.*

1.61 _____ Sucre fought more freedom battles for Ecuador and Bolivia than Bolívar.

1.62 _____ San Martín died a happy man.

1.63 _____ The conquering Spaniards allowed Creoles to be their deputies.

1.64 _____ Pizzaro did not find all the Inca cities.

1.65 _____ Since democracy, no more trouble has bothered the three Indian countries.

Complete this activity.

The following words are from the section on the history of Ecuador, Peru, and Bolivia. Each of these words has a suffix. Classify these words a. in the first column by underlining the suffix; b. in the second column by writing the root word; c. in the third column by describing the root word as a noun, verb, adjective, or adverb; d. in the fourth column by describing the word with the suffix as a noun, verb, adjective, adverb, or a verb with changed tense. The first one is done for you.

	Word	Root Word	Root Word Description	Word With Suffix Description
	civilization	civilize	verb	noun
1.66	conqueror			
1.67	historian			
1.68	centered			
1.69	irrigation			
1.70	government			
1.71	expedition			
1.72	reminders			
1.73	colonial			
1.74	organized			
1.75	fertilizer			
1.76	freedom			
1.77	dictator			
1.78	defeated			
1.79	national			
1.80	obviously			
1.81	liberators			
1.82	unhappily			
1.83	liberation			

COUNTRY OF ECUADOR

Ecuador is on the west coast of South America. It has three main cities, one main industry, and several small industries.

Location. The mainland of Ecuador is located south of Colombia on the west "hump" of South America. Peru borders it on the east and south. To the west is the Pacific Ocean. The Galápagos Islands, which belong to Ecuador, are six hundred miles west in the Pacific Ocean.

Cities. Quito, built on Inca ruins in the north *Sierras*, is the capitol of Ecuador. Because its location is fifteen miles south of the equator, all-year-around the sun rises at 6 A.M. and sets at 6 P.M. Nearby is Mount Pichincha.

Guayaquil is Ecuador's chief port at the mouth of the Guayas River. The city is four hundred fifty years old, but modern looking. Guayaquil's streets are often said to be paved with chocolate, because cocoa beans are put out to dry in the streets. An Inca Indian chief named Guaya and his wife, Quil, killed themselves when the Spanish took over. The conquerors named the city after them.

Cuenca, located in the south *Sierras*, is famous for making fine Panama hats. Men everywhere used to wear these hats, but they are no longer the style. The women of the city continue making them and storing them. They say people will start buying them again someday. Cuenca has marble buildings made from marble from nearby quarries.

Tourists flock to the town of Otavalo in northern Ecuador to buy fine weavings brought to market by the Otavalo women.

Resources and industry. Ecuador's chief resource and industry is bananas. The coastline has the perfect climate for banana growing. Ecuador also exports small amounts of coffee, rice, and sugar. Cocoa used to be a major crop, but a **blight** struck its leaves in 1922. Recovery has been long and slow.

 Answer these questions.

1.84   What country lies to the north of Ecuador? _____

1.85   What islands in the Pacific Ocean belong to Ecuador? _____

_____

1.86   How far to the west do these islands lie? _____

1.87   What is the capital city of Ecuador? _____

1.88   What is the chief port of Ecuador? _____

1.89   The chief port lies at the mouth of what river? _____

1.90   What is Ecuador's chief resource and industry? _____

_____

COUNTRY OF PERU

Peru is below Ecuador on the west coast of South America. Some places have become important tourist stops. Peru has several productive industries.

Location. Peru lies south of Florida on the west coast of South America. Colombia and Ecuador border it on the north. Brazil is to the east, Bolivia the southeast, and Chile to the south.

Cities. Lima is the capital of Peru. A statue of San Martín stands in the central plaza of the city. Presidential guards dress as Europeans dressed long ago.

Callao is located about halfway down the coast of Peru. Callao is so close to Lima that the two have almost grown together into one big city. If you were to travel to Lima by boat, you would get off at Callao, because it is closer to the ocean.

Cuzco was the capital of the Inca empire. Much of Cuzco today is modern, though they do not have much wealth. Many of the buildings have been built on top of the ruins of the old Inca buildings.

Iquitos, in the Oriente, to the northeast is Peru's "Atlantic seaport." Many of its people live in stilt houses as it is located on the Amazon River, which flows into the Atlantic Ocean. Airplanes carry people to and from the city.

Resources and industry. Sugar is grown along the coastline of Peru and in the Amazon valleys. Cotton is also a major crop on the coast.

In the mountains, llama, alpaca, vicuña, and sheep are raised for wool. Gold and silver are still in the hills, but copper, zinc, and vanadium (an element used in hardening steel) are more important. Peru is the world's second largest producer of vanadium. Iron and oil also are produced.

Sugar refining is a major industry. From sugar pulp comes *babazzi* from which paper is made. Textile factories for making cloth from both cotton and wool are major industries. Mining is a major occupation.

Match these words and phrases.

1.91 _____ Cuzco

1.92 _____ Lima

1.93 _____ textile factories

1.94 _____ Peru

1.95 _____ Florida

1.96 _____ sugar refining

1.97 _____ Callao

a. directly north of Peru in the United States

b. capital of Peru

c. capital of the Inca empire

d. Peru's "Atlantic seaport"

e. port city for Lima, Peru

f. world's second largest producer of vanadium

g. a major industry

h. produce cotton and wool cloth

COUNTRY OF BOLIVIA

Bolivia is one of two countries in South America without a seacoast. The cities of importance are those in which the government is located and those that are essential to mining. Bolivia has several agricultural products, mining products, and manufactured products. Bolivia exports some of these.

Location. Peru and Chile form Bolivia's west border. Brazil surrounds it to the north, east, and southeast.

Cities. La Paz, located to the northwest on the central Cordillera, was founded in 1548. The city has no fire department because the plateau is so high that not enough oxygen is present in the air to keep a fire going. Although La Paz is not the capital of Bolivia, most government affairs are run from this city.

Sucre is the legal capital of Bolivia, but only the judicial branch of the government operates there. Located in Sucre is the *Casa de la Independencia* where tourists can see the Bolivian Declaration of Independence. This city is located on the Central Cordillera several miles south of La Paz.

Potosí was a "boom" town in the early mining days because of its location near Cerro Rico (rich hill). This mountain was full of gold and silver that the Pizzaro conquerors took to send to their greedy kings in Europe.

Resources and industry. Tin is the most important metal being mined in Bolivia today. Processing it is the country's chief industry. Cerro Rico is full of tin, as are many of the other mountains. Other important mineral resources are copper, silver, and some gold.

Potatoes and barley are important crops. Rubber and cinchona (quinine) trees are found in the Oriente. Quinine is used in some medicines.

In the high plains are livestock: sheep, llama, alpaca, and vicuña. Next to tin processing, textile manufacture of woolen products is chief in importance.

Complete these statements.

1.98 Bolivia is one of two countries in South America without a _____ _____ .

1.99 Peru and Chile form Bolivia's _____ border.

1.100 The country that surrounds Bolivia to the north, east, and southeast is _____ .

1.101 The legal capital of Bolivia is _____ .

1.102 The most important metal mined and processed in Bolivia today is _____ .

Complete this map activity.

1.103 Place the cities named in this section on the map in the back of your LIFEPAC. Be sure you put on the map all the cities for Ecuador, Peru, and Bolivia. There are eleven altogether.

Complete this writing assignment.

1.104 Choose one of these cities. Look up all the information you can find about it. Then write two or three paragraphs about the city of your choice. If you prefer, you may write about any subject in the study of Ecuador, Peru, and Bolivia you wish. If you prefer a subject besides a city, check with your teacher before you start your research.

Teacher check _____

Initial   Date

Match the words and phrases.

In the column on the left are words or phrases that present an idea. Match each with the idea that contrasts. Write the contrasts in the right-hand column. To contrast means to present an opposite or different point of view.

1.105 _____ greedy kings		a. missionaries
1.106 _____ green jungles		b. died unhappily
1.107 _____ ancient ruins		c. poor people
1.108 _____ rich conquerors		d. today's cities
1.109 _____ fine highways		e. equator
1.110 _____ great liberators		f. crumbling modern walls
1.111 _____ strong Inca foundations		g. no schools to attend
1.112 _____ Go to school		h. no vehicles with wheels
1.113 _____ written language		i. word-of-mouth legends
1.114 _____ coast of Peru		j. coast of Ecuador
1.115 _____ Indians without Christ		k. democratic presidents
		l. barren deserts

Review the material in this section to prepare for the Self Test. The Self Test will check your understanding of this section. Any items you miss on this test will show you what areas you need to restudy.

SELF TEST 1

Write *true* **or** *false* (each answer, 1 point).

1.01 _____ It has been easy for all the countries we have studied in this LIFEPAC to become democracies.

1.02 _____ Bolivia is crossed by the equator.

1.03 _____ The Galápagos Islands are right off the shore of Ecuador.

1.04 _____ The Atlantic seaport on the Amazon, called Iquitos, is in Peru.

1.05 _____ Lake Titicaca is too small for ships.

1.06 _____ Lake Titicaca is on the border between Peru and Bolivia.

1.07 _____ The coastline of Ecuador is fertile.

1.08 _____ The "Avenue of Volcanoes" is in Ecuador.

1.09 _____ All the volcanoes are now inactive.

1.010 _____ Peruvians use the horse to carry things.

1.011 _____ The coastline of Peru has a very dry, cool climate.

1.012 _____ The coastline of Bolivia is mountainous.

1.013 _____ Charqui is the same as jerky.

1.014 _____ The Andes mountain range reaches its widest point in Peru.

1.015 _____ The *altiplanos* are in Bolivia and Peru.

1.016 _____ The llama is a cousin to the giraffe.

1.017 _____ Colombia lies to the north of Ecuador.

1.018 _____ Texas in the United States lies directly north of Peru.

1.019 _____ Cuzco is the port city for Lima, Peru.

1.020 _____ Mount Cotopaxi is called the highest "steaming" mountain in the world.

Write the letter for the correct answer on the line (each answer, 2 points).

1.021   Most of the people in Ecuador, Peru, and Bolivia are _____ .
a. Americans   c. Indians
b. Europeans   d. mulattos

1.022   The men of the Colorado Indian tribe _____ .
a. dye their hair red   c. wear bright ponchos
b. are headhunters   d. eat raw fish

1.023   The Auca Indians of the jungle _____ .
a. are friendly   c. blow darts of poison
b. raise sheep   d. killed five missionaries

1.024   The Indians who make fine woven textiles are _____ .
a. the Capaya   c. the Otavalo
b. the Jivaro   d. the Auca

1.025   Many children do not attend school because _____ .
a. they haven't money for clothes
b. they do not want to
c. they do not have to
d. parents do not want schools.

1.026   Wool in Peru comes from _____ .
a. llamas   c. jaguars
b. jungle plants   d. nutrias

1.027   Along the coastline of Peru there is much _____ .
a. sand skiing   c. mountain climbing
b. baseball   d. pole-vaulting

1.028   Potatoes originally came from _____ .
        a. Peru   c. United States
        b. Ireland   d. China

1.029   The women of Cuenca still make Panama hats because _____ .
        a. they are in style   c. the government says so
        b. somebody will buy them   d. their husbands say so
           someday

1.030   Tapioca comes from the _____ .
        a. manioc plant   c. squash plant
        b. potato plant   d. cornstalks

1.031   The name of the Indians who are descended from the Incas is

        _____ .
        a. Urus   c. Quechuas
        b. Colorados   d. Aymaras

1.032   The women of Bolivia often carry _____ .
        a. crochet work   c. embroidery
        b. spindles   d. mending

1.033   In Bolivia men wear *chullos,* which are _____ .
        a. caps with flaps   c. knitted socks
        b. beanies   d. belts

1.034   A woman wears more skirts in Bolivia to show she is _____ .
        a. poorer   c. married
        b. nicer   d. wealthier

1.035   People in Bolivia make musical instruments out of _____ .
        a. pots and pans   c. reeds and bamboo
        b. tree bark   d. combs

1.036   In Bolivia, because of few textbooks, the teacher reads to the class, and
        the children _____ .
        a. tape the lessons   c. copy on the blackboard
        b. write down and memorize d. never take tests

Match the words and phrases (each answer, 2 points).

1.037 _____ Lima   a. capital of Inca Empire
1.038 _____ La Paz   b. legal capital of Bolivia
1.039 _____ Quito   c. chief port of Ecuador
1.040 _____ Cuzco   d. capital of Peru
1.041 _____ Sucre   e. where most of Bolivia's
1.042 _____ Guayaquil   government is conducted
                               f. capital of Ecuador

Write the words in the blanks that will make the statements correct (each answer, 3 points).

1.043   The Incas expected everybody to pay homage to the _____ .

1.044   Pizzaro captured the _____ nation.

1.045   The Spanish wanted riches to be sent to _____ .

1.046   Some presidents of the Indian countries were democratic, but others became cruel _____ .

1.047   Ecuador's chief export product is _____ .

1.048   Incas had not yet learned about the _____ .

1.049   Incas built their buildings of large _____ .

1.050   Incas put _____ plating on their buildings.

1.051   The liberator of the southern half of South America was _____ _____ .

1.052   Peru is the world's second largest producer of _____ .

1.053   The general who fought more battles to free Ecuador and Bolivia than Bolívar was _____ .

1.054   The most important metal now being taken from Cerro Rico and other mountains in Bolivia is _____ .

Possible Score   100
My Score   _____
Teacher check   _____
                Initial   Date

II. URUGUAY AND PARAGUAY

Uruguay and Paraguay are divided by a narrow strip of Argentina. The names of these two countries are similar. Their geographies are somewhat the same. Almost everything else about the two countries is different. Uruguay has a seacoast, Paraguay does not. Both countries raise cattle but they differ in history and people. Uruguay has much social welfare. Paraguay, because of many costly wars, has a small population.

SECTION OBJECTIVES

Review these objectives. When you have completed this section, you should be able to:

1. Describe the geography of Uruguay and Paraguay.
2. Give an account of the background and the lifestyle of the people in each country.
3. Relate how each country was started and how it has grown to the present.
4. Name the capital of each of the countries and at least one more city.
5. Name the principal resource or resources of each country and the major industries that have grown from these resources.

Restudy these words.

despot	initiate	repeal
estuary	isolate	urban
guerrilla	leisure	

URUGUAY

Uruguay is *gaucho* country. *Gaucho* country means *cowboy country*. Large rangelands provide food for many heads of cattle. The weather is moderate to cold, with only about 120 sunny days a year. Its history includes being occupied by Spain, Brazil, England, and Argentina. Uruguay has helped its people so much that it spent nearly all its money. Now the country needs more income.

Geography. Mostly a flat land, Uruguay is on the Atlantic seacoast south of Brazil and east of Argentina. Four major regions or areas divide it. Along the Coastal Plain are sandy beaches. Rising immediately from the coast are the famous purple Highlands. Red flowers blend with the color of the soil to give the entire area this appearance. West of the Highlands are two low mountain ranges. The south range is the Cuchilla Grande. North and west is Cuchilla de Haedo. Between the two ranges lies the wide valley of the Negro River.

Uruguay owns Lobos Island off its Atlantic coastline. No humans live there, only seals, sea lions, and other water animals.

Many waterways are important to this country. The Rio de la Plata divides part of Uruguay from some of eastern Argentina. Wrongly called a river, it is an **estuary**, which is a wide and long river mouth. Several rivers empty into the Plata and on into the Atlantic Ocean.

The Plata, 170 miles long, is 137 miles wide where it meets the Atlantic. The Paraná and Uruguay are the major rivers that form the Plata by flowing into it.

In the center of the country, on the Negro River, a power dam has been built. The largest man-made lake in South America forms behind this dam. The Yi is another large river in the center of the country. The Uruguay River marks the country's west border.

Wildlife includes the black-necked swan, one of Uruguay's prettiest birds. Nutrias are raised for fur. Water hogs and unusual rabbits abound. Fish of many species are important both for recreation and for food. Fur seals and penguins live on Lobos Island.

Write the correct answer in the blanks.

2.1   Uruguay's weather is moderate to _____ .

2.2   The number of sunny days per year is about _____ .

2.3   Uruguay is on the a. _____ coast, south of b. _____ , and east of c. _____ .

2.4   The huge estuary that divides part of Uruguay from eastern Argentina is the _____ .

2.5   The power dam that forms the largest man-made lake in South America is on the _____ .

2.6   The Uruguay River marks the country's _____ border.

People. Uruguay is the second smallest of the countries of South America. All of its areas are inhabited. Even so, a large portion of the population lives in or around the capital city of Montevideo, located on the wide mouth of the Plata. Along the Atlantic seacoast many resort towns have been developed for the use of the tourists who come to Uruguay to get away from the cold winters in the Northern Hemisphere. Only about 18 per cent of the residents make their homes in rural areas. Most of the people are of European or American descent: Italian, British, German, Hungarian, French, and Spanish.

Uruguay's official language is Spanish.

Schooling is very good in Uruguay. Montevideo has built numerous schools. In rural areas, where schools cannot be built, often a school-on-wheels is set up in a trailer or a bus. All government schools, from kindergarten through university, are free. Nearly everyone can read and write. Even radio lessons are available for those who cannot attend school.

A four- or five-day work week with early retirement has become a fact in Uruguay over the years. Most of the people have a great amount of **leisure** time. Symphonies and other orchestras, social clubs, and country clubs are popular. Soccer games, boat races, and swimming at the beaches are other forms of recreation.

True freedom of religion is enjoyed in Uruguay. Besides the Roman Catholic Church, Anglican (Episcopal),

Methodist, and Jewish groups are there. The Salvation Army has been active for a long time, and so has the YMCA.

Uruguayans eat better than anyone else in South America. They consume two hundred ninety pounds of meat per person each year. The principal drink is a herb tea called *yerba mate.* Brewed from the leaves of the yerba tree, it is often served in a gourd with silver straw. Sometimes in the later afternoon yerba mate is served with cookies. The Uruguayans do not eat the evening meal until nine or ten o'clock at night.

So plentiful have cattle been in Uruguay that the walls of primitive houses used to be made of cowhides. Trees are scarce. Often fences were built of cattle bones.

Uruguay's modern low-cost housing projects for the poor and elderly people have been copied by other countries.

The *Gauchos,* or cowboys, are an important tradition to Uruguay. Most of them are Indian-white mix by birth. Today they work on large ranches, but in the early days they caught wild cattle to sell, or broke wild horses, in the remote grasslands. Their dress was baggy pants with leather leggings, a style that remains today. Their chief hunting tool is a *boleadora* or *bola.* These tools are made by tying stones to leather thongs that are then tied to a longer strip of leather. When the bola is thrown the thongs will wrap securely around any prey.

Gauchos are South American cowboys.

Complete this map study.

2..7

On a separate piece of paper, try to draw a larger map of Uruguay. Mark on it by coloring, or other means, the Coastal Plain, the Highlands, the Cuchillas, and the Negro River valley. Be sure to put in Negro River, showing location of the dam, also the Uruguay, and Paraná rivers. Label the Plata estuary and Lobos Island.

Teacher check _____

Initial   Date

HISTORY & GEOGRAPHY

606

LIFEPAC TEST

80/100

Name _____

Date _____

Score _____

HISTORY & GEOGRAPHY 606: LIFEPAC TEST

Write *true* **or** *false* (each answer, 1 point).

1. _____ Mutton is meat from sheep.
2. _____ Cuzco exhibits many of Argentina's historical relics.
3. _____ The most southern part of Chile is known as the "land of the twilight night" because the sky still glows at midnight.
4. _____ Lobos Island is known for fur seals and penguins.
5. _____ In Paraguay heaviest frost comes in December.
6. _____ Paraguayan women are famous for their spider-web fishing nets.
7. _____ The Spanish killed the Incas and took their wealth.

Write the letter for the answer on the blank (each answer, 2 points).

8. A bird found in the high places of the Andes is a _____ .
   a. condor   c. mockingbird
   b. sparrow   d. parrot
9. The women of Bolivia often carry _____ .
   a. needlepoint   c. spindles
   b. mending   d. crochet
10. The metal now found in Cerro Rico, in Bolivia is _____ .
   a. gold   c. copper
   b. silver   d. tin
11. Many social welfare programs can be found in _____ .
   a. Paraguay   c. Ecuador
   b. Argentina   d. Uruguay
12. The beast of burden that is more or less the unofficial animal of Peru is _____ .
   a. the camel   c. the llama
   b. the horse   d. the elephant
13. Peru's coast has no rainfall because of the _____ .
   a. hot sun   c. bad winds
   b. Peru current   d. no clouds

14. The Inca city that Pizzaro did not find is called _____ .
    a. Kiki
    b. Machu Picchu
    c. Bora Bora
    d. Quechua Quechua
15. The liberators of South America were _____ .
    a. the Jesuits
    b. the Mennonites
    c. San Martín and Bolívar
    d. Perón-Perón
16. The War of the Pacific was fought over _____ .
    a. silver and gold
    b. copper and vanadium
    c. nitrates and fertilizer
    d. palm trees
17. Textile factories make _____ .
    a. paper
    b. oil
    c. cloth
    d. bagezzi
18. Adding -ation to the verb civilize changes the word to _____ .
    a. a noun
    b. an adjective
    c. a preposition
    d. an adverb
19. In Bolivia the Andes form into _____ .
    a. three cordilleras
    b. four cordilleras
    c. two cordilleras
    d. two orientals

Write one fact about each of these cities (each answer, 3 points).

20. Cuenca _____
21. Filadelfia _____
22. Salto _____
23. Primavera _____
24. Cuzco _____
25. Tucamán _____

Write the correct answer from the list in the blank (each answer, 2 points).

meat	altiplanos
gaucho	wars
Magellan	Lake Titicaca
O'Higgins	earthquakes

26. The population of Paraguay is low because of many costly _____
    _____ .

27. The name of the famous explorer whose crew mutinied by Argentina was
    _____ .

28. The body of water important in legends of both Boliva and Peru is _____
    _____ .

29. The people of Uruguay and Argentina eat a lot of _____ .

30. Chile often has to remake its maps because of _____ .

31. A man in Chile who helped San Martín was _____ .

32. A _____ is the South American cowboy.

33. The name of the high plateaus that form a region between mountains in Bolivia
    is _____ .

Name the seven countries studied in this LIFEPAC and name their capitals.
One country has two capitals (each 2-part correct answer, 5 points).

Name	Capital
34. a. _____	b. _____
35. a. _____	b. _____
36. a. _____	b. _____
37. a. _____	b. _____
38. a. _____	b. _____
39. a. _____	b. _____
40. a. _____	b. _____

Match the words and phrases.

2.8	_____ meat	a.	hunting tool
2.9	_____ Lobos Island	b.	spare time
2.10	_____ nutrias	c.	coastline
2.11	_____ Montevideo	d.	fur
2.12	_____ estuary	e.	government schools
2.13	_____ resorts	f.	Plata
2.14	_____ free	g.	favorite drink
2.15	_____ fences	h.	where most of the population of
2.16	_____ four-day week		Uruguay live
2.17	_____ *yerba mate*	i.	low cost housing project
2.18	_____ *gaucho*	j.	fur seals
2.19	_____ *boleadora*	k.	cowboy
		l.	290 pounds per person
		m.	cattle bones

History. Explorers looked along the South American Atlantic coast for a water passageway across the continent to the Pacific. This influenced the growth of Uruguay. In 1517 Juan Díaz de Solís discovered the Plata estuary. He thought this might be the passage he was looking for. He started up its wide mouth but was killed by savage Indians before he could explore it. A few years later Sebastian Cabot also found the Plata. His scouts were killed by Indians. Further efforts to explore the estuary were forgotten until many years passed and the Indians became more friendly under the influence of priest-missionaries.

After two hundred years, Spain took control of Uruguay in 1777. Thirty years later, in 1807, the British occupied the country for a brief seven months. This period was long enough for them to introduce a printing press. They printed papers about democracy that were handed out to all people. In 1827 after another twenty years, the British intervened again. This time they freed Uruguay from Brazil and Argentina.

In 1830 Uruguay's first constitution was adopted. Two parties were formed, but, unfortunately, war broke out between them.

During the seventy-three years between 1830 and 1903, twenty-five presidents headed Uruguay. Only three of them had peaceful terms. All of the others were involved in assassinations or revolutions or were forced out of power.

José Batlle y Ordóñez, called Batlle (Bawt´ yay), a newspaperman-journalist, was elected president of Uruguay for the term 1903 to 1907 and again in 1911 to 1915. He **initiated** the secret ballot, so that each person could vote in private. He insisted that all children go to school, and that there be schools for them. He formed labor unions which led to the short work weeks and early retirements. He thought government should be run by a committee instead of one person. A committee-government law was finally enacted in 1951, but it was **repealed** fifteen years later.

Dr. Oscar Gestido came to office in 1967, fifty-two years after Batlle. By this time the social reforms of Batlle were resulting in problems. Uruguay was not exporting enough goods, or earning enough money other ways, to be able to do all the things it wanted to do for its people. Many officials were dishonest. Dr. Gestido started a stern economy program. He died after nine months, but his successors have carried out his ideas.

Today Uruguay is a country with promise. Its people are happy and live well, but it needs better ways to earn money. The constitution, restored in 1985, provides for free elections. Julio Sanguinetti was elected president in 1994.

Since 1962, bands of **urban guerrillas** have blown up radio stations, robbed banks, and have, by many activities, caused unrest in Montevideo. Nobody knows exactly what these men have in mind, nor is it possible to know when they will strike again.

Cities. Small cities are scattered all over Uruguay. Along the coastline are the tourist resorts.

Montevideo is the main city and capital around which the country's business centers. The city has an old section where the government buildings are, a central modern part, and the suburbs, full of lovely homes. There are no slums.

Colonia is a city by the Plata, north and west of Montevideo. Many historical landmarks are there.

Salto is north by the Uruguay River, in gaucho country. Salto, too, is a town that attracts many tourists.

Resources and industry. Uruguay's chief resource and industry is livestock. This includes, of course, the important cattle industry.

Hernando Arias de Saavedra, commonly known as Hernanderias, is considered the first gaucho. In 1603 he brought cattle and horses into the grasslands of Uruguay and let them run wild. Other gauchos began to do the same thing, thus making the country's cattle industry as large as it is now.

Sheep raising comes second in export value. Almost all of the country's land is usable, at least for grazing. Meat packing has grown as a source of income. In the ocean are whales, sought by British, Scandinavian, and Russian fishermen. Sealing on Lobos Island is important, too. The third largest industry in Uruguay is tourism (taking care of pleasure-seeking travelers). Most of the food now grown is used within the country. Uruguay looks forward to expanding its fruit and vegetable exports. Exporting fruit may be a new way to earn much needed income.

Write *true* **or** *false*.

2.20 _____ Early explorers along the Atlantic coast were looking for good beaches.

2.21 _____ Indians killed many of the explorers and their men.

2.22 _____ The first gaucho brought cattle and horses to run wild in the grasslands.

2.23 _____ The British never had control of Uruguay.

2.24 _____ The first efforts for democracy were through printed papers.

2.25 _____ When two parties were formed in the new republic, all became peaceful.

2.26 _____ During Batlle's presidency the five-day work week started.

2.27 _____ Batlle wanted to rule the country all by himself.

2.28 _____ Gestido started an economy program.

2.29 _____ Urban guerrillas keep law and order like city policemen.

Do this activity.

2.30 Circle the names of the cities of Uruguay mentioned in your LIFEPAC, and find them on a map. There are three of them plus the coastal resorts. Write the names of the three cities and add one fact about each.

2.31 _____ _____

2.32 _____ _____

2.33 _____ _____

Teacher check _____
                        Initial   Date

Write a word or phrase for each of these words that describes its importance to Uruguay.

2.34 livestock _____

2.35 meat packing _____

2.36 sealing _____

2.37 whales _____

2.38 grazing _____

2.39 travelers _____

2.40 vegetables _____

2.41 tourism _____

PARAGUAY

Paraguay is the least populated conutry in South America. The vast majority of the population consisits of Guarani Indians. The government has encouraged immigrants to settle in order to build up the population.

Geography. Paraguay is divided in two by the Paraguay River. To the east of the river are flat plateau lands where most of the country's farming is done. To the far east are rolling hills. West of the river lies the Chaco area, which has few inhabitants.

This area is part of the Gran Chaco (great swamp) of South America.

More black-spotted leopards roam in the Paraguayan Chaco than anywhere else. Also many insects abound, such as the malaria mosquito, as well as boring gnats and ants that dig into the soles of the feet.

The whole country is hot, up to 100 degrees in summer. It never snows in winter. Sometimes it frosts in June which is a winter month south of the equator.

The Paraguay River joins the Pilcomayo River at the point of the city of Ascunción.

The joined rivers flow southward to join the Paraná River at the extreme southern tip of the country. These rivers give Paraguay an outlet to the Atlantic Ocean.

People. Fewer people live in Paraguay than in any other country of South America. Wars have killed many of the men. Half of the population is under twenty years of age.

A Japanese settlement at Ydytymi is not far from Ascunción. Hutterites (a religious group) have made their home at Primavera, to the west of the Paraguay River. A large, old colony of Mennonites migrated to Filadelfia (Colonia Mennonita) in the center of the Chaco.

The Guarani Indians make up the greater portion of the population. Though Spanish is the official language, 90 per cent of the people speak their Guarani dialects with pride.

Schools are free, and children from seven to fourteen are required to attend. Most children do. The country has a severe lack of teachers.

Women make beautiful spider-web lace and hand-embroidered clothes. Men do leather tooling, wood carving, pottery, and jewelry.

Each day from noon to three o'clock is *siesta,* or rest time. The Paraguayans have many forms of recreation, but they are especially fond of music. Native orchestras are made up of three guitars and a kind of harp.

Complete this map study.

2.42   On your work map in the back of this LIFEPAC put in the Paraguay River that divides Paraguay in half. To the east show plateaus, and rolling hills farther east. To the west of the river, show the Chaco. You may want to color these areas. Add the Pilcomayo and Parana rivers.

Teacher check _____
                                    Initial   Date

Write *true* or *false* in the blank in front of each statement.

2.43 _____ It frosts in June in Paraguay because June is a winter month there.

2.44 _____ No farming is done in the flat plateaus.

2.45 _____ The Paraná River gives Paraguay an outlet to the Atlantic Ocean.

2.46 _____ It is crowded in Paraguay because of booming population.

2.47 _____ Most people there are over 65 years of age.

2.48 _____ Wars have killed many men in Paraguay.

2.49 _____ Most of the people are Guarani Indians.

2.50 _____ The people work from morning to late night without rest.

2.51 _____ Spider-web lace, made by Paraguayan women, is beautiful.

2.52 _____ Paraguayan orchestras have pipe organs.

History. The early Guarani Indians were mostly farmers. Their peace was shattered when Spaniards began to search for gold. Sebastian Cabot, an Englishman exploring for Spain came first. Ascunción was founded by explorers in 1537 and it became the center of all settlements along the Plata. The Jesuit missionaries worked kindly with the jungle Indians for one hundred fifty years here.

In 1813 the Paraguayans managed to separate themselves from all other countries. They adopted their own constitution. José Gaspar de Francia was elected Perpetual Dictator in 1815. He served for twenty-five years. He was a cruel man who **isolated** Paraguay from the rest of the world. He kept no records.

In 1841 Carlos Antonia López became president. He also was a despot, but a kind one. He established schools, freed the slaves, and built the first railroad in South America. He appointed his son Francisco to be his successor.

In 1862 Francisco López took over and continued much of his father's work. His lack of ability got Paraguay into the Triple Alliance War with Brazil and Argentina. Two-thirds of the Paraguayans were killed in this war. United States President Rutherford B. Hayes finally was asked to settle the boundary dispute. He gave all disputed areas to Paraguay.

In the eighty-four years from 1870 to 1954 thirty-nine presidents were elected. Internal unrest kept most of them from serving full terms. The Gran Chaco War with Bolivia from 1934 to 1937 increased the land holdings of Paraguay, but it cost them the lives of thirty-two thousand soldiers.

From 1934 to 1989 General Alfredo Stroessner was president of Paraguay. He calmed the country. During his term, the Trans-Chaco Railroad was built. Also, in cooperation with Brazil, a huge hydroelectric plant on the Paraná River was constructed. It was named the Itaipu Dam Power Plant and began generating electricity in 1984.

Juan Carlos Wasmosy was elected Paraguay's first civilian President in 1993.

Cities. Surrounded by seven hills, Ascunción is the capital and largest city in Paraguay. Its streets are named for leaders or dates in history. Many plazas with fine old hotels, such as the Hotel Guarani, and a botanical garden make the city beautiful. Primavera (springtime) is the Hutterite community. The residents are well known for their handmade items.

Encarnación was an old Jesuit village. When a tornado destroyed it, a new city was built. Filadelfia, the Mennonite city, is full of industrious farmers, who run cooperative stores and markets.

Resources and industries. Over half of the people in Paraguay live and work in rural areas—on farms, cattle ranches, or timberland. Cattle ranching is first in economic importance. Lumber is next in importance. The lumber business includes the making of the wood by-product, tannin. Agriculture is third. Some of the products grown for home use or export are yerba mate, manioc, sugar, pineapples, and cotton.

Industries include textile mills, sugar mills, and oil refineries. In recent years the country has been assembling cars and tractors for American companies. Paraguay also pasteurizes milk as an industry.

A primitive lumber wagon for hauling logs out of the Gran Chaco

---

Answer these questions about these Paraguayan leaders and their ideas.

José de Francia	Carlos López	Francisco López	Alfredo Stroessner
dictator	dictator	dictator	peacekeeper
cruel	kind	power-hungry	dictator
power-hungry	good worker	war leader	good worker

2.53   Which dictators were most alike in a positive way?

_____

2.54   Which dictators were most alike in a negative way?

_____

Complete this map study.

2.55   Circle the names of four cities in Paraguay mentioned in the paragraph about them.

2.56   Place the names on your work map.

Teacher check _____
                            Initial   Date

Write at least one fact about each city.

2.57   Ascunción _____

2.58   Encarnación _____

2.59   Primavera _____

2.60   Filadelfia _____

Complete this writing assignment.

2.61   Choose one of these items from Paraguay or Uruguay

yerba mate	Mennonites	boleadoras or bolas
gauchos	Hutterites	jungle insects

or you may choose any city or historical person.
Look up information on the subject you have chosen.
Write two or three paragraphs about your choice.
Get your teacher's approval of your choice before you proceed. Write your report on a separate sheet of paper.

Teacher check _____
                            Initial   Date

Review the material in this section to prepare for the Self Test. The Self Test will check your understanding of this section and will review the first section. Any items you miss on this test will show you what areas you need to restudy.

SELF TEST 2

Write *true* **or** *false* (each answer, 1 point).

2.01   _____   *Gaucho* means *jerked meat.*

2.02   _____   Uruguay has much social welfare.

2.03   _____   The shoreline of Peru is green and fertile.

2.04   _____   Uruguay is on the Pacific seacoast.

2.05 _____ Paraguay and Uruguay have no high mountains.

2.06 _____ In Paraguay there are gnats that bore into the skin.

2.07 _____ The highlands of Uruguay look purple.

2.08 _____ The Amazon River gives Paraguay an outlet to the Atlantic
Ocean.

2.09 _____ Paraguay is divided into two parts by the Negro River.

2.010 _____ In Paraguay it sometimes frosts in June.

2.011 _____ The Plata is not a river but an estuary.

2.012 _____ The Plata divides Paraguay from Argentina.

2.013 _____ Uruguay has many beaches.

2.014 _____ Lobos Island is a favorite resort for tourists.

2.015 _____ A power dam is on the Negro River.

2.016 _____ The Paraguay River divides Paraguay in two.

2.017 _____ A despot is a tyrant.

2.018 _____ *Leisure* means *free time from regular work.*

2.019 _____ The word urban is related to cities.

2.020 _____ Guerrillas are persons engaged in irregular warfare.

Match the words and phrases (each answer, 2 points).

2.021 _____ Lobos Island   a. active in Uruguay

2.022 _____ mobile schools   b. *siesta* time

2.023 _____ Mennonites   c. Hutterites

2.024 _____ Primavera   d. drink from a gourd with
                                                  a silver straw
2.025 _____ Guarani Indians
                                               e. Paraguay
2.026 _____ *boleodoras*
                                               f. swamp
2.027 _____ noon to 3 p.m.
                                               g. leather thong tools
2.028 _____ Salvation Army
                                               h. much leisure time
2.029 _____ Chaco
                                               i. three guitars and a harp
2.030 _____ fences
                                               j. in the Chaco
2.031 _____ Paraguay native orchestras
                                               k. free
2.032 _____ baggy pants and leggings
                                               l. textile mills
2.033 _____ *yerba mate*
                                               m. seals and sea lions
2.034 _____ copied by other countries
                                               n. Uruguay rural areas
2.035 _____ four- to five-day work week
                                               o. cattle bones
2.036 _____ Uruguay government schools
                                               p. gaucho

                                               q. Uruguay's low-cost housing

Name these cities (each answer, 3 points).

2.037   Name the capital of Uruguay. _____

2.038   Name the city in the Chaco that the Mennonites built. _____

_____

2.039   Name the capital of Paraguay. _____

2.040   Name the town in Uruguay that is in gaucho country.

_____

Complete the statements by writing the correct word or words in the blank.
(each answer, 3 points).

2.041   A country we are studying noted for its tourist resorts is _____

_____ .

2.042   *Yerba mate* is made from the leaves of _____ .

2.043   Potatoes originated in _____ .

2.044   *Altiplanos* are _____ .

2.045   The Incas made their buildings of _____ .

2.046   Lake Titicaca is between Peru and _____ .

2.047   Uruguay's chief resource and industry is _____ .

2.048   Uruguay hopes to grow more _____ for income.

2.049   The _____ introduced the printing press to Uruguay.

2.050   The principal drink in Uruguay is _____ .

2.051   A huge hydroelectric plant was built on Paraguay's _____
River.

2.052   The United States President who settled a boundary dispute in Paraguay
was _____ .

	Possible Score	100
	My Score	_____
	Teacher check	_____
		Initial Date

III. ARGENTINA AND CHILE

Argentina and Chile fill the bottom third of the South American triangle. Here the continent stretches down deep into the Atlantic and Pacific oceans nearly as far as the polar region. Argentina, to the east, looks like a large beefsteak. Chile runs like a long, narrow bone down the western coastline. The Andes mountains divide the coastline. Argentina's north region is an **extension** of the Gran Chaco in Paraguay. Chile's *norte* (north) is desert, like the coast of Peru.

SECTION OBJECTIVES

Review these objectives. When you have completed this section, you should be able to:

1. Describe the geography of Argentina and Chile.
2. Give an account of the background and the lifestyle of the people living in each country.
3. Relate how each country was started and how it has grown to the present.
4. Name the capitals of each country and at least one more city.
5. Name the principal resource or resources of each country and the major industries that have grown from these resources.

Restudy these words.

conflict	historical	porcelain
extension		

ARGENTINA

Most of the people of Argentina are European. The cities are modern. In the center and to the north, the land is green and grassy; the south is bleak and windy. Like many countries in South America, Argentina has an unsettled history.

Geography. In northern Argentina, the Paraná River cuts through the Chaco on its way out to the Plata estuary. East of the Paraná River is a bent fingerlike stretch of land (about the size of California) running up beside Uruguay and Brazil. This land is called Mesopotamia. Mesopotamia's east border is the Uruguay River. The Uruguay enters the Plata near Buenos Aires. The

central region is the Pampas, full of fertile plains. Here much of the beef and grains of the country are grown. The River Colorado divides the Pampas from Patagonia. The Patagonia region extends south to remote, barren areas. It comes to a tip at the Strait of Magellan. Constant drought and blowing winds make this area fit only for raising sheep. Deep south, below the Strait of Magellan, is the three-cornered tip of Argentina called Tierra del Fuego. This land, too, is sheep-raising country. The Falkland Islands off Argentina's southeast coast are owned by England.

People. Comparatively few Indians live in Argentina now because they were pushed back and killed in the 1800s. The fights between the white men and the Indians there resemble the Indian wars of North America. Today the population is mainly Spanish, Italian, and English.

Argentina celebrates two days in September, a "Day of the Students" and a "Day of the Teacher." Teachers and students alike wear white smocks to elementary school. Private and public schools are both under government control.

Food, clothing, and houses are all much like those found in the United States. Since Argentina is cattle country, the people eat much meat.

The country's main church is the Roman Catholic Church. Church holidays are celebrated. Pan-American Day and other national holidays are also observed.

Spanish is the official language of Argentina.

Complete this map study.

a. Paraná River   g. Andes
b. Mesopotamia   h. Tierra del Fuego
c. Patagonia   i. Gran Chaco
d. Pampas   j. Colorado River
e. Strait of Magellan   k. Atlantic Ocean
f. Uruguay River

3.1   Classify these names according to the location of each in Argentina.

East	West	North	Central	South

3.2   On the map in the back of your LIFEPAC, add the regions, mountains, rivers, and other waterways in Argentina.

Write *true* **or** *false.*

3.3 _____ Argentina never has had many Indians.

3.4 _____ Students and teachers in Argentina wear white smocks to school.

3.5 _____ The Falkland Islands off Argentina's south coast are owned by England.

3.6 _____ The early Argentine fights with the Indians were similar to the Indian wars in the United States.

3.7 _____ Most Argentineans eat fruit and vegetables only.

3.8 _____ Argentina residents wear distinctly native dress.

3.9 _____ A "Students Day" and a "Teachers' Day" are celebrated in Argentina.

History. First to come to Argentina were the explorers, Solís and Sebastian Cabot. Both have been previously mentioned in this LIFEPAC. Many others also helped open up Argentina.

Ferdinand Magellan sailed around the south coast of Argentina in 1520. He was having trouble with the crews of his nearly worn-out ships. They landed on a south shore and were greeted by Indians wearing huge fur shoes. The men called this place Patagonia, after the Spanish word meaning *big feet.* Magellan's fleet limped on through the Strait of Magellan on its way to China.

In 1536 a village of mud huts by the Plata was established by Don Pedro de Mendoza. This early town was destroyed by Indians and was rebuilt in 1580 by Juan de Garay. Today it is known as Buenos Aires.

After Napolean defeated the king of Spain, the Spanish viceroy in Buenos Aires was ousted. A junta of citizens set up its own government in 1810.

In 1812 José de San Martín began his activity for liberation of Argentina. He would disguise himself as a peasant walking on the docks in order to observe the movements of the Spanish ships in the Buenos Aires harbor. When the Spanish were ready to attack, San Martín and his men were prepared. Once, the leader's horse was killed beneath him. A young soldier shielded the pinned-down San Martín with his own body and shouted, "I die without regret. We have beaten the enemy!" Immediately a Spaniard ran a bayonet through the boy. Actually the Spanish were defeated easily. Then San Martín and his followers made an almost impossible march across the high Andes to free Chile and Peru. He sacrificed his life funds for the cause of freedom. But Argentineans never quite trusted his motives. He died a heartbroken man.

Through the years Argentina has had many leaders. Some were cruel dictators, some were democratic leaders. In 1946 a man named Juan Domingo Perón took over. He was charming, but became a dictator. His wife, Eva, did much to help the poor. She was loved by everyone. Like her husband, she used everything she did for the people to gain power for herself. She died of cancer at the age of 33. Perón was overthrown in 1955. He came back in 1973 with a new wife, Isabel. They both won the presidency on a Perón—Perón election ticket. Perón was old and died in 1974. Isabel, as vice-president, tried to hold the country together but could not. Argentina in 1978 was under the military leadership of a president elected from the ranks of army officers. In 1982 Argentina seized the Falkland Islands from the British. But the British sent a full sea and air task force, winning back the islands quickly. In 1983, civil unrest led to the return of free elections, and in December of 1983, a freely elected president and congress took office.

President Carlos Saúl Menem was elected to office in 1989.

Fernando de la Rua was elected president in 1999, but resigned amid rioting and civil chaos in December 2001. Others briefly held office after de la Rua's departure, and President Eduardo Duhalda was elected January 1, 2002. The country continues in civil and economic unrest.

Answer these questions.

3.10   Why was the Spanish viceroy ousted? _____
_____

3.11   How was it possible for San Martín to observe the Spanish fleet of ships in the Buenos Aires harbor? _____
_____

3.12   Why did the Argentineans treat San Martín so badly? _____
_____

3.13   How many times did Juan Perón become president of Argentina?
_____

3.14   Who was more popular with the Argentine people than Perón himself?
_____

3.15   Why do you think she was more popular? _____
_____

3.16   How was it possible for Isabel Perón to gain control of Argentina after her husband died? _____
_____

3.17   What do we mean by saying Argentina is now under military leadership?
_____

Complete this writing assignment.

3.18   Look up information on Ferdinand Magellan. Write, in full sentences, two or three paragraphs about him. Be sure to include in this report who he was, why his sailors mutinied, his final destination, and how South America is important in his story.

Teacher check _____
                          Initial   Date

38

Cities. Buenos Aires, the capital of Argentina, is a big, bustling city located by the Plata estuary. Changeable and crowded, it has costly mansions and lowly slums.

About a thousand miles north and west of Buenos Aires is Tucamán, which used to be an important colonial city. "Casa Historica" (**historical** house) is a museum in Tucamán that holds many of Argentina's documents.

San Julián is the city on the south coast where Magellan's men began to mutiny. Córdoba is an industrial center located in the north-central Pampas region.

Resources and industry. Argentina's industry is centered mainly in Córdoba, although many other cities have factories, too. The first South American jet airliners were manufactured here. Today, cars and trucks also are manufactured.

Livestock is an important industry. In the green Pampas, cattle are raised. From the bleak Patagonia, and even bleaker Tierro del Fuego, sheep, and the wool from them, are exported.

Oil and petroleum products are gaining importance as exports. Grains and other agricultural products are exported also.

Match the words and phrases.

3.19 _____ Pampas

3.20 _____ Buenos Aires

3.21 _____ Tierro del Fuego

3.22 _____ Córdoba

3.23 _____ Tucamán

3.24 _____ San Julián

3.25 _____ exports

a. oil, petroleum products, agricultural products

b. sheep and wool exported

c. costly mansions and lowly slums

d. Magellan's men began to mutiny

e. cattle are raised

f. Patagonia

g. industrial center in north-central Pampas region

h. "Casa Historica"

Complete this map activity.

3.26   Circle the names of cities in Argentina in the text of your LIFEPAC. Then write them on your working map.

Teacher check _____

                                Initial   Date

CHILE

The country of Chile is so narrow and rugged that it appears almost as if it were ready to fall off the coast of southwestern South America. Earthquakes often are so severe that parts of the terrain disappear into the Pacific Ocean. Nevertheless, the friendliness of Chile's people is solid, and their pride in their country is sincere. All the wealth of the country is owned by a few people. The unequal distribution of wealth causes much political unrest. Its cities, however, are busy with commerce and industry.

Geography. Chile's long strip of land is no more than two hundred miles at its widest point. Looking from east to west, first are the high Andes Mountains, then a central valley, followed by a high plateau, after which the land goes down into the Pacific Ocean. At the southern tip of the country the central valley disappears. The mountains become lower.

Regions from north to south are (1) the *Norte Grande* and the *Norte Chico* (big north and small north.) No rain falls here; this area is a long desert. The Peru current sweeps past this part of the coast as it does past Peru. Continuing southward, the land gradually becomes green as one approaches the central valleys. (2) The Central Region is where most of the people live. Rain falls only in winter. The south-central part of this region used to be thick with forests. Many of the trees have been taken out, but much timber still remains. (3) The Southern Region is noted for earthquakes. Sometimes the earth moves so much that new maps have to be drawn. It rains in the Southern Region any time of the year. The far south is more bleak and windy. Chile's tip is near the South Polar region. This far south is known as the "land of the twilight night" because the sky at midnight still glows.

Chile's rivers all flow directly from the Andes to the Pacific. The three most important rivers are the Bío Bío River to the south, the River Aconcagua in the Central Region, and the River Loa near the Bolivian border.

Wildlife includes sea lions and large ocean fish. Sea animals such as penguins and otters abound off the coasts. Inland are found sheep, vicuña, and guanacos, both wild and tame. Many varieties of wild flowers cover the plateaus.

Write *true* **or** *false.*

3.27 _____ The earthquakes in Chile never amount to much.

3.28 _____ Chile and Argentina almost extend to the region of the South Pole.

3.29 _____ All rivers in Chile flow from north to south.

3.30 _____ South Chile is called "the land of the twilight night" because electricity comes on at suppertime.

3.31 _____ Chile is no more than two hundred miles wide at its widest point.

3.32 _____ Many varieties of wild flowers grow in Chile.

3.33 _____ From east to west in Chile, you would go over high Andes mountains, a central valley, a high plateau, and a sharp descent into the Pacific Ocean.

3.34 _____ Norte Grande and Norte Chico are very wet.

People. In the early days of Chilean history, the Araucanian was the largest tribe of Indians. They intermarried with the Spanish frequently enough so that most of the population today is made up of mestizos. When migrations from Europe began, the English were the first to arrive in Chile. The English influenced the clothing of the people. German immigrants taught the army the "goose step" way of marching. Most colonial settlers, however, were Spanish, some of them coming from the country of the Basques in Spain.

Today children from seven to fourteen are required to go to school. The courses are so difficult that many drop out. Out of a hundred students only twenty finish sixth grade. The rural areas often do not have enough schools or enough teachers.

Chileans go to the beaches often. No one lives far from a beach. Skiing in the mountains is popular, too. Soccer and rodeos are favorite sports.

Independence Day is celebrated September 18. Christmas is a summer holiday in Chile (as it is in all of South America) because Chile is south of the equator. The children show much devotion to the baby Jesus.

Most people belong to the Roman Catholic Church, but many other religious groups are also active in Chile.

Chileans have an afternoon tea because they do not eat supper until 9 p.m. Rural homes have homemade cheese and fresh hot bread. For Christmas they might eat turkey or sea crabs or even eels. In some areas mutton (meat from sheep) is served several times a day.

Spanish is Chile's official language. French and English often are second languages.

Write antonyms for these words.

3.35 wide _____ 3.40 heavy _____

3.36 south _____ 3.41 many _____

3.37 disappear _____ 3.42 rural _____

3.38 gradually _____ 3.43 winter _____

3.39 approach _____ 3.44 lower _____

                                    3.45 goes _____

Match the words and phrases.

3.46 _____ Spanish   a. mountains

3.47 _____ mutton   b. evening meal

3.48 _____ seven to fourteen   c. go to the beaches

3.49 _____ skiing   d. homemade cheese and hot bread

3.50 _____ rodeo   e. official language

3.51 _____ 9 p.m.   f. summer holiday

3.52 _____ rural meal   g. favorite sport

3.53 _____ Christmas   h. meat from sheep

                                  i. required to go to school

---

History. Chile suffered from the conquests of Pizzaro and his partner, Almagro, as did the northern South American countries. Chile had less of the riches they wanted, however, so its problems were less severe than those of the countries in the north. In the early years, pirates also roamed the coastline.

In the 1700's Chile established a regular postal service. Mule trains were routed over the Andes to Buenos Aires.

When San Martín came to Chile in 1817, he was helped by a man named Bernardo O'Higgins, whose father was an Irish pioneer leader. O'Higgins became the Supreme Director of Chile. He was almost a dictator, but he tried to improve conditions in Chile. He started schools, irrigation, food markets, and sewers in Santiago. He printed books and periodicals. In 1823 he was exiled to Peru.

Chile's two political parties were always at war with one another. The country was involved in the War of the Pacific, over nitrates, with Peru and Bolivia. As in other countries, some presidents of Chile served well, and some were caught up in **conflicts**.

In Chile at the present time, three-fourths of the land belongs to 2 per cent of the people. This inequality causes much unrest. Another problem is the control of Chile's rich resources by corporations from the United States and other foreign countries.

Dr. Salvador Allende had first attempted to become president of Chile in 1958. In 1964 his second attempt was defeated by Eduardo Frei. Eduardo Frei then had Chile buy its own huge copper interests back from an American company. This should have helped the country to gain economic independence, but other foreign corporations owned other resources.

In 1980, a constitution was adopted allowing for a more democratic government. The once abolished Congress has limited legislative power and in 1993, Eduardo Frei was elected president.

On one of the high Andes mountains is a statue of Christ. It signifies friendship between Argentina and Chile. Argentina and Chile still have many misunderstandings between them. The Bible says, Psalm 34:14 ". . . do good; seek peace, and pursue it." Perhaps the people of South America are learning that peace has to be truly desired. All efforts, by every person, have to be turned in the direction of peace. Then, with the help of God, peace, instead of war, can rule.

Cities. Santiago, located in the Central Region, is the capital of Chile. Every year Santiago has a solemn procession on May 13 to remember its 1647 earthquake. All the government offices and much of the country's industry are in Santiago.

Directly west of Santiago is Chile's second largest city, Valparaiso. Chile's biggest commercial centers are there.

Valparaiso is a very international city, very much influenced by the British. In the far north, the port city of Antofagasta has the country's school of mines.

Concepción, south of Valparaiso, has the largest harbor in Chile. This city houses the country's chief naval base.

Valvidia, farther south near the coastline, is built on islands. Modern schools of forestry and medicine make this city famous. Many artists and writers gather there.

Resources and industry. Copper is Chile's chief mining product, but the country is also rich in silver, iron, manganese, coal, and nitrates. Many people work in mines. As explained in a previous paragraph, most of the minerals are controlled by big companies in the United States, Great Britain, and other countries.

Chile has several factories for steel and copper processing. Besides these, glassmaking factories, **porcelain** factories, paper mills, flour mills, and textile industries employ many people.

 Put these words and phrases in the order in which they happened.

3.54	_____	military government
3.55	_____	pirates
3.56	_____	San Martín
3.57	_____	sewers in Santiago
3.58	_____	Chile buys back copper mines
3.59	_____	Pizzaro and Almagro
3.60	_____	Bernardo O'Higgins
3.61	_____	Allende
3.62	_____	regular postal service
3.63	_____	Frei
3.64	_____	War of the Pacific

Complete these sentences by writing the correct answer in the blank.

3.65   The chief mining product in Chile is _____ .

3.66   Big businesses mainly in a. _____ and b. _____
_____ control some of the mines in Chile.

3.67   Five other industries in Chile are a. _____ ,
b. _____ , c. _____ , d. _____ ,
and e. _____ .

Do this writing assignment.

3.68   Look up in encyclopedias, magazines, books, or any other resource,
information about Chile's earthquakes. After you get your information,
write two or three paragraphs about what you have learned. Use a
separate piece of paper for this project.

Teacher check _____
                        Initial   Date

Complete this map activity.

3.69   On the work map in the back of your LIFEPAC add these Regions: a.
North or Norte, b. Central, and c. Southern. Shade in with colored pencil
or crayon and put a color guide on one side.

3.70   Locate these rivers on the work map: a. Bio Bio, b. Aconagua, c. Loa.

3.71   Circle the names of the cities mentioned in your LIFEPAC, then put them
on your map: a. Santiago, b. Valparaiso, c. Concepción, d. Valvidia, e.
Antofagasta.

Teacher check _____
                        Initial   Date

Before you take this last Self Test, you may want to do one or more of these self checks.

1. _____ Read the objectives. See if you can do them.
2. _____ Restudy the material related to any objectives that you cannot do.
3. _____ Use the SQ3R study procedure to review the material:
   a. **S**can the sections.
   b. **Q**uestion yourself.
   c. **R**ead to answer your questions.
   d. **R**ecite the answers to yourself.
   e. **R**eview areas you did not understand.
4. _____ Review all vocabulary, activities, and Self Tests, writing a correct answer for every wrong answer.

SELF TEST 3

Write *true* or *false* (each answer, 1 point).

3.01 _____ The capital of Argentina is Córdoba.

3.02 _____ Quito is the capital of Ecuador.

3.03 _____ San Julián, on Argentina's coast, is where Magellan's men mutinied.

3.04 _____ Cuzco in Peru was the Inca capital.

3.05 _____ The capital of Chile is Santiago.

3.06 _____ Concepción, Chile, has a naval base.

3.07 _____ Tucamán exhibits many of Argentina's historical relics.

3.08 _____ Sucre in Bolivia was named after one of Bolívar's generals.

3.09 _____ The city in Ecuador named after two Indians is Guayaquil.

3.010 _____ The capital of Uruguay is Montevideo.

3.011 _____ The Galápagos Islands are off the coast of Chile.

3.012 _____ The rivers of Chile all run east to west.

3.013 _____ In Ecuador the "Avenue of Volcanoes" is a street in Quito.

3.014 _____ *Conflict* means *fight* or *struggle*.
3.015 _____ The llama is related to the camel.
3.016 _____ The "land of the twilight night" means Chileans leave their lights on all night.
3.017 _____ The Andes reach their widest point in Bolivia.
3.018 _____ Earthquakes in Chile are often very bad.
3.019 _____ The Peru, or Humboldt, current is in the Atlantic Ocean.
3.020 _____ *Abound* means a *little rabbit*.

Match the words and phrases (each answer, 2 points).

3.021 _____ homemade cheese and hot bread   a. Argentina
                                          b. Peru's coast
3.022 _____ Auca Indians   c. meat from sheep
3.023 _____ friendly   d. very hard in Chile
3.024 _____ British   e. goose-step marching
3.025 _____ mutton   f. Indian-Spanish mix
3.026 _____ Germans   g. dried meat
3.027 _____ mestizo   h. from Spain
3.028 _____ school courses   i. soccer
3.029 _____ hardy Basques   j. people living in high Andes
3.030 _____ *futbol*   k. influenced Chile's clothes
3.031 _____ large chests, lungs   l. Mennonites
3.032 _____ jerky   m. people of Chile
3.033 _____ spindles   n. women of Bolivia
3.034 _____ Filadelfia   o. rural meal in Chile
3.035 _____ "Student Day"   p. turning to Christ

Write the letter for the correct answer on the line (each answer, 2 points).

3.036   There are few Indians in Argentina because _____ .
     a. they were killed
     b. they died in famine
     c. they never were there
     d. they migrated elsewhere

3.037   All students and teachers in Argentina wear _____.
- a. shirt and tie
- b. European dress
- c. uniforms
- d. smocks

3.038   The Indian tribe in Ecuador called "the red ones" is _____

_____ .
- a. the Capayas
- b. the Navajos
- c. the Aucas
- d. the Colorados

3.039   The official language of all countries we have studied in this LIFEPAC is

_____ .
- a. Portuguese
- b. English
- c. Spanish
- d. Indian dialects

3.040   The gauchos wear _____ .
- a. baggy pants and leggings
- b. derby hats
- c. chaps and levis
- d. bolas

3.041   The country in this LIFEPAC with the smallest population is _____

_____ .
- a. Uruguay
- b. Bolivia
- c. Chile
- d. Paraguay

3.042   Argentine and Chilean people are mostly _____ .
- a. Baptists
- b. Roman Catholics
- c. Mennonites
- d. Episcopalians

Write the correct answer in the blanks (each answer, 3 points).

3.043   Argentina is divided from Chile by the _____ .

3.044   The region in Argentina named after "big feet" is _____ .

3.045   The small three-cornered area at the extreme south of Argentina is ____
_____ .

3.046   On Argentina's pampas grow _____ .

3.047   The river that cuts through Argentina's Chaco on its way to the Plata is
_____ .

3.048   Argentina's Mesopotamia is about the size of _____ .

3.049   The Galápagos Islands are owned by _____ .

3.050   Lake Titicaca is the highest _____ lake in the world.

3.051   The chief export of Ecuador is _____ .

3.052   The city in Argentina where jet airliners, cars and trucks are manufactured is _____ .

3.053   Sheep are raised in the _____ region of Argentina.

3.054   Chile is no more than _____ wide.

Possible Score   100

My Score   _____

Teacher check   _____
                Initial   Date

Before taking the LIFEPAC Test, you may want to do one or more of these self checks.

1.   _____   Read the objectives. See if you can do them.
2.   _____   Restudy the material related to any objectives that you cannot do.
3.   _____   Use the SQ3R study procedure to review the material.
4.   _____   Review activities, Self Tests, and LIFEPAC vocabulary words.
5.   _____   Restudy areas of weakness indicated by the last Self Test.

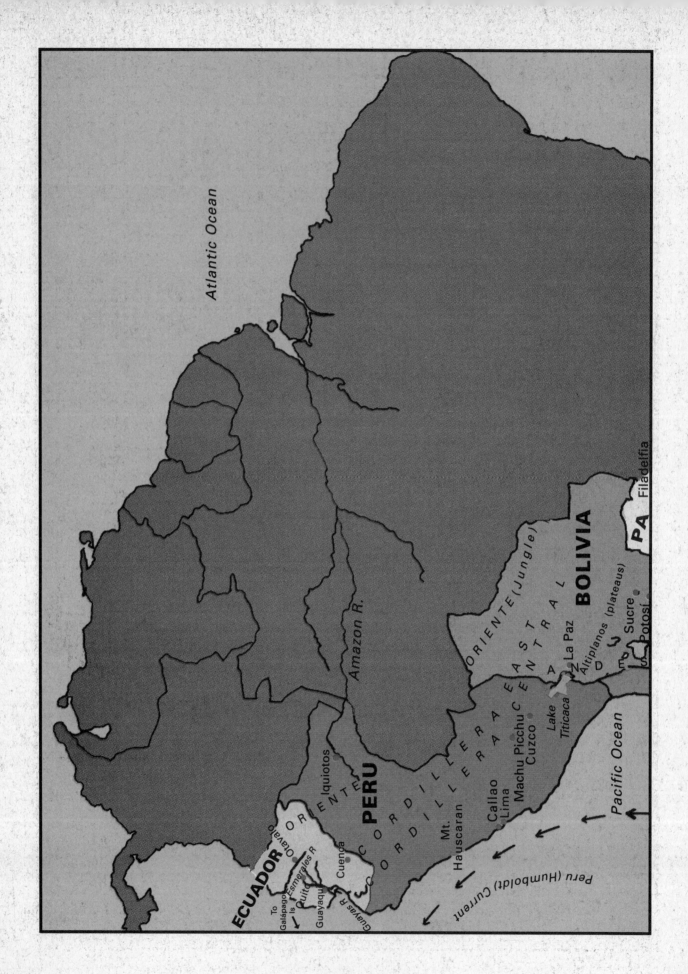

Atlantic Ocean

ECUADOR

Otavalo

To Galápago Is.

Quito

Esmeralas R.

Guayaquil

Guayas R.

Cuenca

Iquiotos

ORIENTE

CORDILLERA OCCIDENTAL

PERU

Amazon R.

Mt. Hauscaran

Callao
Lima

Machu Picchu
Cuzco

CORDILLERA CENTRAL

Lake
Titicaca

ORIENTE (Jungle)

CORDILLERA EASTERN

ANDES

La Paz

Altiplanos (plateaus)

BOLIVIA

Sucre

Potosí

PA

Filadelfia

Pacific Ocean

Peru (Humboldt) Current

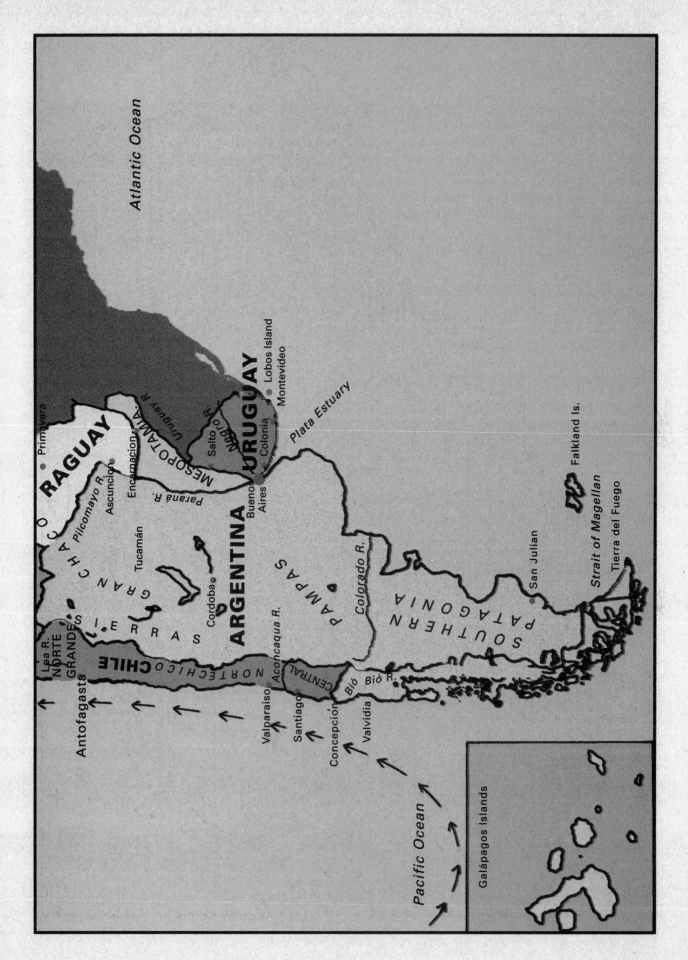

Atlantic Ocean

Primavera

RAGUAY

CHACO

GRAN CHACO

Pilcomayo R.

Ascunción

Encarnación

MESOPOTAMIA

Uruguay R.

Salto R.

Negro R.

Paraná R.

Tucamán

Córdoba

SIERRAS

NORTE GRANDE

Lpa R.

Antofagasta

CHILE

NORTE CHICO

Valparaiso

Santiago

Concepción

Valvidia

Aconcagua R.

CENTRAL

Bío Bío R.

ARGENTINA

PAMPAS

Colorado R.

URUGUAY

Lobos Island

Montevideo

Colonia

Buenos Aires

Plata Estuary

SOUTHERN PATAGONIA

San Julian

Falkland Is.

Strait of Magellan

Tierra del Fuego

Pacific Ocean

Galápagos Islands

50